WIRE WRAPPING JEWELRY
TECHNIQUES FOR BEGINNERS

A Basic Guide to Learning How to

Make Wire-Wrapped Jewelry

Copyright@2022

Prince Brighton

Table of contents

CHAPTER 1

INTRODUCTION TO WIRE WRAPPING

Wire-wrapping is one of the earliest jewelry-making techniques, dating back thousands of years before the Common Era. Components are created using jewelry wire and related findings (such as headpins) using this technique. Then, wire components are joined together mechanically, without soldering or heating. Typically, after being shaped into a loop or some other decorative form with a pair of pliers, a wire is completed as a wire component by being wrapped around itself. Because of this, the decorative shape or loop will remain in place. This type of craft gets its name from the method of wrapping wire around itself, which is known as **wire wrapping.**

Wire wrapping techniques are seldom utilized in mass-produced jewelry because machines can cast (mold) jewelry components more quickly, affordably, and precisely. Individuals predominantly use the wire-wrapping technique to create jewelry.

The primary distinctions between wire-wrapped jewelry and other jewelry-making techniques are twofold;

1. Wire wrapped jewelry is composed of wire and sometimes wire-like findings (head-pins, jump rings, etc.)

2. The components of wire-wrapped jewelry are mechanically connected to one another rather than being joined together through soldering or other forms of heat treatment. A mechanical connection involves interlocking two loops to create a link between them.

An integral component of wire-wrapped jewelry is a wire loop. To create mechanical connections between components, loops are joined together.

A "P" loop is created by bending the wire till it re-contacts itself (but this is too crude looking for serious jewelry use). The most attractive loop is the eye loop, which has a complete wire circle centered on the wire stem (like a lollipop).

P and eye loops are examples of "open" loops. This would imply that the loop can be opened up mechanically in order to allow it to link to a different component;

however, this also means that it can open too quickly when it is subjected to strain. A "wrapped loop" is a stronger (and more attractive) loop in which the end of the wire is wrapped around the stem of the loop three or four times to ensure that the loop cannot be opened. A link must be made between two wrapped loops before the second loop is closed.

In the simplest instance of handcrafted wire-wrapped jewelry, a bead is strung onto a head–pin, a jewelry-making finding. The "head" of the head pin holds the bead in place. The section of the head pin that emerges from the opposite side of the bead is composed primarily of wire. Using hand tools, this wire is bent into a loop and the excess is cut off. The resultant bead suspended from a loop is referred to as a "bead dangle." The loop on the bead dangle is attached to the loop at the end of the ear wire finding to make a basic earring.

CHAPTER 2

BASIC WIRE WRAPPING TOOLS

In the fabrication of wire-wrapped jewelry, four basic tools are needed and several others are beneficial.

Wire Cutters

The wire cutters are easy to operate and are an excellent choice for cutting wires of a range of diameters.

Round Nose Pliers

Round nose pliers have conical jaws and are used to create loops in wire.

Flat Nose Pliers

Flat nose pliers are exactly as their name suggests; they are flat on both inner sides and are used to keep regions flat or bend wire at 90-degree angles.

Chain Nose Pliers

Chain nose pliers feature flat, smooth jaws and are used to grab and bend wire.

Note

Nylon jaw pliers, a ruler, a chase hammer, bench block, loop closing pliers, and a jewelry making jig are also useful tools for making wire-wrapped jewelry.

Wire

Wire is available in round, square, and half-round shapes, as well as flat and pre-twisted designs. In addition to this, it is obtainable in a variety of materials. Wires made of copper and brass are particularly simple to manipulate and shape.

Copper wire can be thinly hammered. Brass wire is slightly more rigid than copper wire, yet it is quite easy to manipulate. The sterling silver is malleable yet retains its shape nicely once it has been shaped. A layer of 12- or 14-karat gold is bonded to a support material to produce gold-filled wire. In a similar fashion, silver-filled wire is manufactured through the same process, and the connection between the two materials is permanent.

The diameter of wire, which is expressed by gauge numbers, is used to determine its size.

The thicker the wire, the smaller the gauge will become.

Wire Gauge

A 12- or 14-gauge wire is relatively heavy, but perfect for constructing bracelets and chokers.

10-gauge wire is quite thick and brittle.

26-gauge wire is nearly as fine as hair (this tiny wire is suitable for coiling embellishments).

16-gauge wire can be used to create jump rings and necklace and bracelet links.

18-gauge wire can be used to add embellishments and create finer links.

Types of Wires

Memory Wire is a pre-coiled, stiff wire that makes it simple to produce rings, bracelets, and necklaces.

Beading Wire is a nylon-coated stranded stainless steel wire. It works well with abrasive beads. A thinner wire will give lightweight beads such as gemstone, liquid gold, or liquid silver, or seed beads an attractive drape. To accommodate larger, heavier bead strands, a heavier gauge wire should be utilized.

Super-thin Beading Wire is a 34-gauge wire that may be shaped and woven around findings. This wire is so tiny that it can fit through nearly any drill hole. Due to its thinness and low tensile strength, it should only be employed with lightweight beads.

Color-Coated Copper Wire (sometimes referred to as Enameled Copper Wire) is a copper-based crafting wire that is soft, very pliable, and relatively good at retaining its shape.

Wire-wrapping, chain-making, and other jewelry creation techniques utilize **precious metal wire**, most frequently sterling silver, fine silver, and gold. There are four shapes available: square, twisted, round, and half-round.

Additionally, precious metal wire comes in three hardnesses:

Dead Soft Wire is highly pliable and can be bent into a number of forms with relative ease. It has poor shape retention at stress places such as clasps.

Half-Hard Wire is bendable, but it retains its complex structure under moderate force. It is useful for weight-bearing wire-wrapped jewelry components.

Full Hard Wire is used for wire-wrapping jewelry because it maintains its shape. It is ideal for clasps due to its tempering and ability to hold delicate motifs. It is more difficult to manipulate than soft or half-hard wire.

PROJECT 1

HOW TO MAKE WIRE WRAPPED AMETHYST CRYSTAL EARRINGS

These amethyst crystal stud earrings are adorable, stylish, and simple to make. This quick little DIY will instantly dress up any looks. It can also be worn as a pendant by omitting the earring hooks.

Supplies Needed

- Amethyst crystal beads (They must have a hole in the top)
- Open earring hooks
- 26 gauge wire
- Wire cutters

- Round nose pliers

- Flat nose pliers

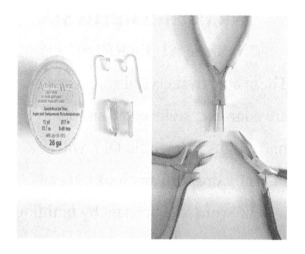

Step 1

First, Prepare the Wire

Start by cutting two pieces of wire of about 6inches in length (This need not be exact, as excess can always be trimmed off at the end).

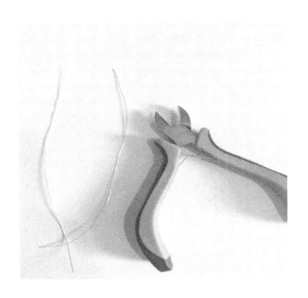

Take one length of wire and construct a loop in the middle, and then twist the wire many times below the loop to complete it. Proceed in the same manner with the second wire piece.

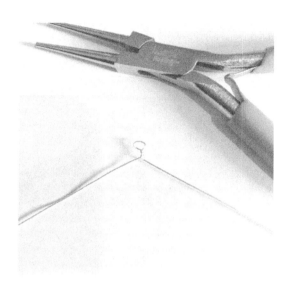

Step2

Wrap the Crystals

Place one of your wire loops on top of a crystal, and then let each wire's tail pass through the crystal hole (you should now have the loop above the crystal with both tails emerging on opposing sides through the hole).

Next, wrap the tail ends around the
top of the crystal until the desired
effect is achieved. Remove any excess
wire and tuck it beneath the wrapped
wire. Repeat with the remaining
crystal and wire loop.

Step 3

Add Earring Hooks

Place the wrapped crystal onto the open earring hook and secure it with pliers to prevent it from falling off.

Continue with the second crystal.

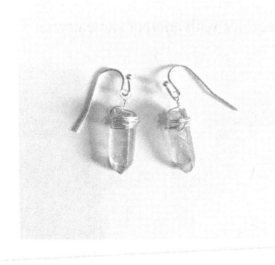

Note

If you would rather create a pendant, simply omit the hooks and string the crystal onto a chain.

Step 4

Here is the finished product of your wire wrapped earrings. So lovely! You could also create a matching necklace with another same crystal.

PROJECT 2

HOW TO MAKE HEAD PIN BRANCH WIRE EARRINGS WITH BEADS

These colorful dangling earrings have a lot of movement when worn due to their dangling nature, but are actually quite simple to create. Depending on the materials used, they can be produced extremely cheaply. Alternatively, you can create a set of pricey, exquisite earrings. By utilizing different head pins and beads, you can simply alter the style.

Supplies Needed

- 10 head pins per pair

- Beads (check that they are able to fit on the head pins) - 10 beads for each pair
- Earrings hooks
- Round nose pliers
- Flat nose pliers
- Wire cutters

Step 1

Create the First Branch

Attach a single bead to a single head pin, and then ensure that the bead do not slip over the head. But if this occurs, it can be remedied by first stringing a seed bead as displayed in the image beneath.

Now use your round-nose pliers; bend the tail end of the head pin about 7-8mm at a 90deg angle.

With the round-nose pliers, form a loop in the "tail," and then use the flat-nose pliers to fine-tune the loop.

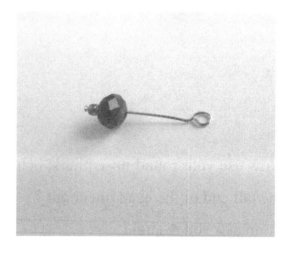

Step 2

Create the Second Branch

Thread a second head pin just in same manner as you did with the first one. Now insert the end of the second head

pin through the newly-formed loop of
the first one.

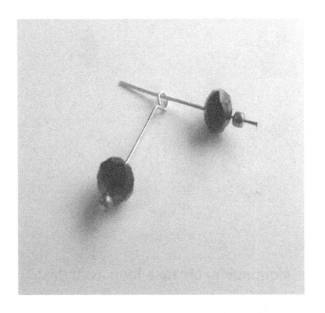

Hold the open end of the second head
pin as the second head pin is still
connected to the first head pin, and
then bend it at a 90deg angle.

Continue to create a loop as in the previous step.

Step 3

The Remaining Branches

Continue creating branches until five head pins have been used.

Note

When the chain of branches is lifted,
they will hang in a zigzag pattern.

Step 4

Add Earring Hook

Grab one ear wire loop with your flat-
nose pliers and twist it to the side to

open it (Just a little twist will be enough).

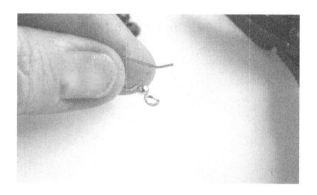

Now connect the final branch loop and then close the earring hook loop. One earring is completed!

Repeat the entire procedure to create a second pair of earrings. Wow here is the completed product, looks great!

PROJECT 3

HOW TO WIRE WRAPPED COPPER PENDANT

Making this pendant may look a little difficult but the following technique used is easily adaptable. This pendant is created with a teardrop-shaped piece of fused glass, but you could also use stone or other things.

Note

1. The technique used for this wire wrapped pendant is applicable to stones of various sizes and shapes.

2. For this wire wrapped pendant, I used pure copper wire but you could use another type of wire if you want.

Step 1

Supplies Needed

- Glass or stone drops
- 16 gauge copper wire
- 24 gauge copper wire
- 2 jump rings (should be of the same material as the wire or simply create these on your own using the 16 gauge wire)
- Wire-cutter
- Round nose pliers
- Flat nose pliers
- Measuring tape

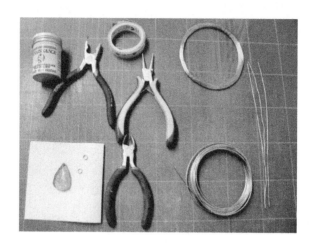

Step 2

Beginning construction of the copper frame

First, measure around the item (stone) you are using. I am using a glass drop which measures 8.5cm.

The value is multiplied by two, plus a bit extra. That is the length of the 16-gauge copper strip that will be used.

I use 20cm (8.5cm x2 = 17cm plus additional 3cm extra) each for the measurement of my copper wire piece.

Cut 3pieces of 16-gauge copper wire strands, straighten them as much as possible and then place them next to one another and indicate the center.

Cut a meter length of 24 gauge wire.

At this point, starting in the center, wind the thinner wire (24g wire) around the three pieces of thicker wire (16g wire) while holding them together. Ensure that the three wires remain parallel and are not bunched together. Wind to a width that will accommodate the base of your stone (about 1cm).

Trim the wire end and flatten it against the thicker wires, ensuring that the beginning and end of the wrapping wire are on the same side. This is the interior of the frame you are constructing.

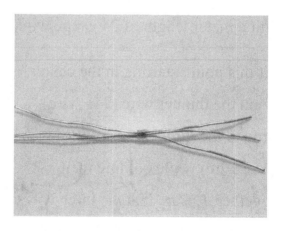

Tip

Rolling wires on a tabletop using a flat board is a simple approach to get them perfectly straight.

Step 3

Proceeding with the Frame

Repeat the previous procedure of winding the thinner wire twice more on either side of the newly-formed center piece. Ensure that the beginning and ending wires of the wrapping are on the same side.

To further tighten the three wrapped sections, squeeze them with the pliers.

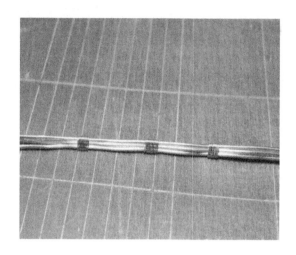

Step 4

Forming the Structure (frame)

Wrap the wires around the stone with care, ensuring that the wire ends are on the inside, against the stone.

Adjust the height of the two wrapped parts on the side by sliding them along the wires to the appropriate position.

I prefer to position one somewhat higher than the other, although symmetry is also okay.

Step 5

Shaping the Structure

Remove the stone from the wires and pull each side's top wire inside with care.

Adjust the wires and reposition the stone as necessary. You may need to slightly push them outside.

Step 6

Remove the stone once more, flip the wires over, and then repeat **step 5** on the opposite side.

The two central wires on either side will remain in their current positions.

Replace the stone and modify the frame wires until you are satisfied with their shape.

Step 7

Securing the Structure

Gather the 6 wires end at the top and tightly wrap them with additional 24-gauge wire. Be sure to tuck the wire's starting between the 16-gauge wires so that it does not protrude.

Working towards the pendant is easier than working away from it.

To complete the pendant, wrap the wire around one side of the pendant a few times further, then trim it and tuck it under the other wires.

Step 8

Front Spiral Finish

Make a little spiral or coil at the end of each wire using the round-nose pliers by bending two wires down over the pendant's front.

As displayed in the image below, adjust the spiral so that one spiral neatly rests beneath the other.

Step 9

Back Spiral Finish

Repeat the preceding step 8 on the
back of the pendant.

I tighten my spirals here to prevent
them from catching on clothing.

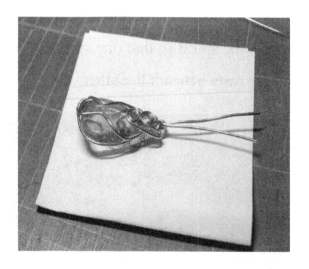

Step 10

Complete Your Pendant

Shorten the final two wires (enough to make one single loop with each).

Using the pliers with a round nose, form a single loop with each wire. I create two parallel loops, but you can alternatively keep them joined.

Insert a jump ring through both hoops, and then use your flat-nose pliers to close the jump ring.

Insert the second jump ring through the first (on the pendant's back) and close it. This is the jump ring through which your chain will pass through!

Congratulations on completing your pendant. Here is the finished product of your pendant.

PROJECT 4

HOW TO MAKE GLASS CRYSTAL BEAD WIRE EARRINGS

How to make wire earrings with a few inexpensive jewelry craft supplies; using inexpensive crystal glass beads to add a strong sense of charm and glitter to the stunning pair of earrings, which are very lightweight and shimmer beautifully!

Supplies Needed

- Black and White Bicone Crystal Glass Beads 4mm
- Round Seed Beads (12/0 2x1.5mm)
- Jewelry Pliers

- Nylon Fishing Thread 0.2mm (eyepin)

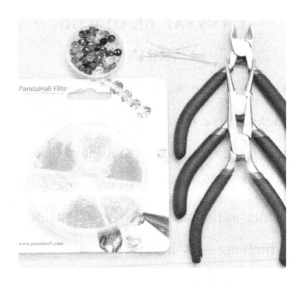

Step 1

Construct Fundamental Black And White Crystal Earrings

1. First, thread five black 4mm bicone beads onto the eyepin and form a loop at the opposite end;

2. Second, thread five white 4mm bicone beads onto the eyepin and form a loop at the opposite end;

3. Thirdly, thread the four bead links onto an eyepin and form a loop at the opposite end.

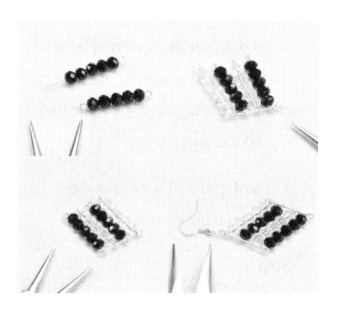

Step 2

Complete the Beaded Dangle Earrings

1. First, thread an eyepin through the loop of the bead links as displayed in the image below.

2. Second, attach an earring hook to the basic beaded dangle, and you have completed one pair of black and white crystal earrings.

3. Third, proceed with the other beaded dangle earring;

Step 3

Done!

The black and white crystal beaded earring has been completed.

Conclusion

The technique of wire wrapping is not difficult and can even be fun; you can begin making your own wire jewelry by beginning with any of the straightforward projects in this book. I really hope that this book will be of the utmost assistance to you, and that it will enable you to begin making wire jewelry. Goodluck!

Made in the USA
Las Vegas, NV
25 January 2024

84804958R00036